Tenor

Young Ladies, Shipmates & Journeys

21 Classical Songs for Young Men Ages Mid-Teens and Up

Compiled by Joan Frey Boytim

ISBN 978-1-4234-3954-7

HAL•LEONARD®
CORPORATION

7777 W. BLUEMOUND RD. P.O. BOX 13819 MILWAUKEE, WI 53213

In Australia Contact:
Hal Leonard Australia Pty. Ltd.
4 Lentara Court
Cheltenham, Victoria, 3192 Australia
Email: ausadmin@halleonard.com.au

T0056148

Visit Hal Leonard Online at
www.halleonard.com

PREFACE

Young Ladies, Shipmates & Journeys is a classical solo book compiled for male voice students whose changed voices have settled into the tenor and baritone/bass ranges. Accompaniments were recorded by Laura Ward for practice for those who use these learning aids.

This volume, containing 21 songs, complements *The First Book of Tenor and Baritone/Bass Solos, Parts I, II,* and *III.* Even without the words, the listener can definitely tell that the songs are masculine in nature.

Included are some easy English folksongs; however, most of the pieces are robust and rhythmical settings of male texts such as "I Am a Pirate King," "Shipmates o' Mine," "The Song of Brother Hilario," "Nothing But a Plain Old Soldier," and "While the Foaming Billows Roll."

The level of difficulty is easy to medium. Most of the tempos are moderately fast. The ranges are very accessible with a top F for the tenors and only a few high E-flats for the baritones/basses.

Many of the song texts use sailor and sea themes in various forms. The texts regarding young ladies are more in the folksong and classical style rather than sentimental love songs, and are easily presented by younger male singers. One is taken on journeys to various ports of call as well as the old road to home. Adult males as well as teenagers will find many of these pieces pure fun to sing, and a chance to express masculinity in song.

Joan Frey Boytim
May, 2008

CONTENTS

ABOUT THE ENHANCED CD

In addition to piano accompaniments playable on both your CD player and computer, this enhanced CD also includes tempo adjustment and transposition software for computer use only. This software, known as Amazing Slow Downer, was originally created for use in pop music to allow singers and players the freedom to independently adjust both tempo and pitch elements. Because we believe there may be valuable uses for these features in other musical genres, we have included this software as a tool for both the teacher and student. For quick and easy installation instructions of this software, please see below.

In recording a piano accompaniment we necessarily must choose one tempo. Our choice of tempo, phrasing and dynamics is carefully considered. But by the nature of recording, it is only one option. Similar to our choice of tempo, much thought has gone into our choice of key for each song.

However, we encourage you to explore your own interpretive ideas, which may differ from our recordings. This new software feature allows you to adjust the tempo up and down without affecting the pitch. Likewise, Amazing Slow Downer allows you to shift pitch up and down without affecting the tempo. We recommend that these new tempo and pitch adjustment features be used with care and insight.

The audio quality may be somewhat compromised when played through the Amazing Slow Downer. This compromise in quality will not be a factor in playing the CD audio track on a normal CD player or through another audio computer program.

INSTALLATION INSTRUCTIONS:

For Macintosh OS 8, 9 and X:
- Load the CD-ROM into your CD-ROM Drive on your computer.
- Each computer is set up a little differently. Your computer may automatically open the audio CD portion of this enhanced CD and begin to play it.
- To access the CD-ROM features, double-click on the data portion of the CD-ROM (which will have the Hal Leonard icon in red and be named as the book).
- Double-click on the "Amazing OS 8 (9 or X)" folder.
- Double-click "Amazing Slow Downer"/"Amazing X PA" to run the software from the CD-ROM, or copy this file to your hard disk and run it from there.
- Follow the instructions on-screen to get started. The Amazing Slow Downer should display tempo, pitch and mix bars. Click to select your track and adjust pitch or tempo by sliding the appropriate bar to the left or to the right.

For Windows:
- Load the CD-ROM into your CD-ROM Drive on your computer.
- Each computer is set up a little differently. Your computer may automatically open the audio CD portion of this enhanced CD and begin to play it.
- To access the CD-ROM features, click on My Computer then right click on the Drive that you placed the CD in. Click Open. You should then see a folder named "Amazing Slow Downer". Click to open the "Amazing Slow Downer" folder.
- Double-click "setup.exe" to install the software from the CD-ROM to your hard disk. Follow the on-screen instructions to complete installation.
- Go to "Start," "Programs" and find the "Amazing Slow Downer" folder. Go to that folder and select the "Amazing Slow Downer" software.
- Follow the instructions on-screen to get started. The Amazing Slow Downer should display tempo, pitch and mix bars. Click to select your track and adjust pitch or tempo by sliding the appropriate bar to the left or to the right.
- Note: On Windows NT, 2000, XP and Vista, the user should be logged in as the "Administrator" to guarantee access to the CD-ROM drive. Please see the help file for further information.

MINIMUM SYSTEM REQUIREMENTS:

For Macintosh:
Power Macintosh; Mac OS 8.5 or higher; 4 MB Application RAM; 8x Multi-Session CD-ROM drive

For Windows:
Pentium, Celeron or equivalent processor; Windows 95, 98, ME, NT, 2000, XP, Vista; 4 MB Application RAM; 8x Multi-Session CD-ROM drive

BARBARA ALLEN

Words traditional

Old English Melody
arranged by
Roger Quilter

Moderato, poco con moto (♩ = 72)

espressivo *mp* *p*

mp In Scar-let Town, where I was born, There was a fair maid

p a tempo

dwell-in', Made ev-'ry youth cry "Well-a-day!" Her name was Bar-b'ra

mp *p*

Al-len. *dolce e grazioso* All in the mer-ry

mf con moto 3 *mp* *delicato e grazioso* 3

6

month of May When green buds they were swel - lin', Young

con tristezza

Jem - my Grove on his death - bed lay For love of Bar - b'ra

con tristezza

più legato   *sonore*

Al - len.

poco appassionato

molto cresc.   *poco dim.*

Ped.   *

p legato

Then slow - ly, slow - ly she came up, And

pochiss. rit.   *p ben legato*

knel - lin', And ev - 'ry stroke the ___ dead - bell gave Cried

"Woe to Bar - b'ra Al - len!"

When he was dead and laid in grave Her

heart was struck with sor - row, "O moth - er, moth - er, ___ make my bed, For

THE BAY OF BISCAY

Andrew Cherry

John Davy

night was drear and dark, Our poor de-vot-ed ___ bark, ___ Till next ___
cling to slip-p'ry shrouds, Each breath-less sea-man ___ crowds, ___ As she ___

day there she ___ lay In ___ the ___ Bay ___ of ___ Bis-cay, O!
lay till next ___ day In ___ the ___ Bay ___ of ___ Bis-cay, O!

3. At length the wished for mor-row Broke ___ through the ha-zy ___ sky, Ab -
4. Her yield-ing tim-bers sev-er, Her ___ pitch-y seams are ___ rent, When

BLACKBIRDS AND THRUSHES

Collected and arranged by
Cecil J. Sharp

Andante affettuoso

1. As
3. Her

I was a-walk - ing for my re - cre - a - tion, A -
cheeks blushed like ro - ses, her arms full of po - sies, She

down by the gar - dens I si - lent - ly strayed, I ____
strayed in the mead - ows and, weep - ing, she said: My ____

heard a fair maid mak - ing great lam - en - ta - tion, Cry - ing:
heart it is ach - ing, my poor heart is break - ing, For

mf

colla voce

Jim - my will be slain in the wars I'm a - fraid.
Jim - my will be slain in the wars I'm a - fraid.

2. The black - birds and
4. When Jim - my re -

thrush - es sang in the green bush - es; The
turned with his heart full of burn - ing, He

wood - doves and larks seemed to mourn for this maid; And the
found his dear Nan - cy all dead in her grave He ___

song that she sang was con - cern - ing her lov - er: O
cried: I'm for - sak - en, my poor heart is break - ing, O

mf

colla voce

Jim - my will be slain in the wars I'm a - fraid.
would that I nev - er had left this fair

dim.

maid! _____

rall.

THE COASTS OF HIGH BARBARY

Collected and arranged by
Cecil J. Sharp

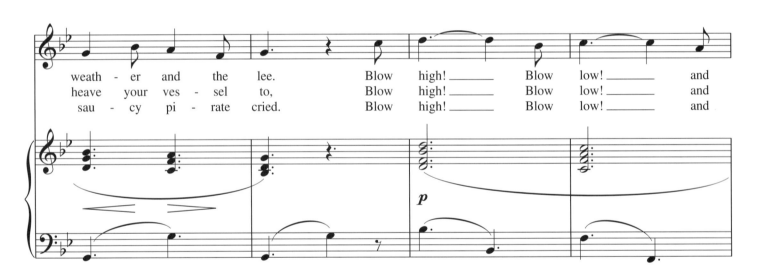

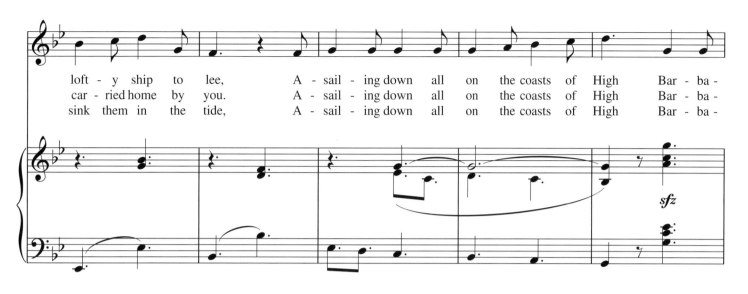

loft - y ship to lee, A - sail - ing down all on the coasts of High Bar - ba-
car - ried home by you. A - sail - ing down all on the coasts of High Bar - ba-
sink them in the tide, A - sail - ing down all on the coasts of High Bar - ba-

ry. 2. Then hail her, our cap - tain he call - ed o'er the side; Blow
ry. 5. We'll back up our top - sails and heave our ves - sel to; Blow
ry. 8. With cut - lass and gun O we fought for hours three; Blow

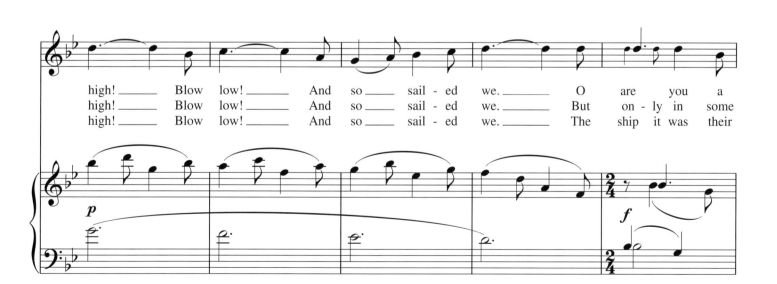

high! Blow low! And so sail - ed we. O are you a
high! Blow low! And so sail - ed we. But on - ly in some
high! Blow low! And so sail - ed we. The ship it was their

pi - rate or ____ a man - o' - war, he cried? A - sail - ing down all
har - bour and ____ a - long the side of you. A - sail - ing down all
cof - fin, and ____ their grave it was the sea. A - sail - ing down all

dim.

on the coasts of High Bar - ba - ry. 3. O are you a
on the coasts of High Bar - ba - ry. 6. For broad - side for
on the coasts of High Bar - ba - ry. 9. But O it was a

mf

pi - rate or man - o' - war, cried we? Blow high! ____ Blow
broad - side, they fought all on the main; Blow high! ____ Blow
cru - el sight and griev - ed us full sore, Blow high! ____ Blow

p

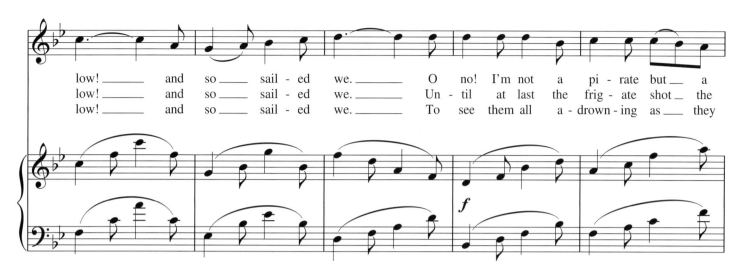

low!_____ and so_____ sail - ed we._____ O no! I'm not a pi - rate but _ a
low!_____ and so_____ sail - ed we._____ Un - til at last the frig - ate shot _ the
low!_____ and so_____ sail - ed we._____ To see them all a - drown - ing as _ they

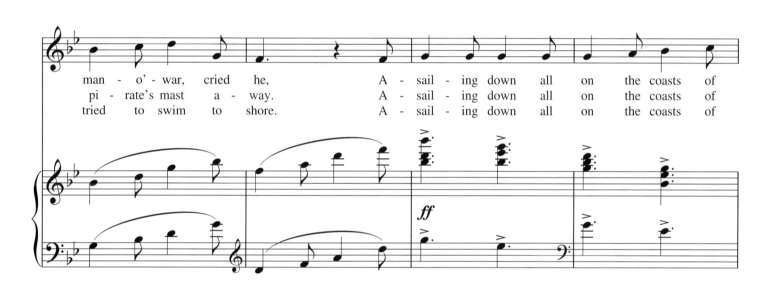

man - o' - war, cried he, A - sail - ing down all on the coasts of
pi - rate's mast a - way. A - sail - ing down all on the coasts of
tried to swim to shore. A - sail - ing down all on the coasts of

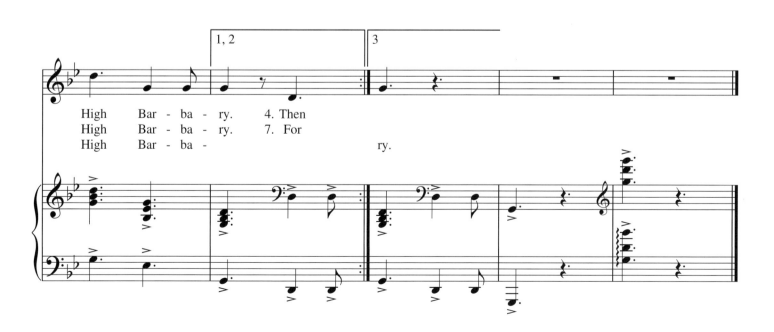

High Bar - ba - ry. 4. Then
High Bar - ba - ry. 7. For
High Bar - ba - ry.

COME LET'S BE MERRY

H. Lane Wilson

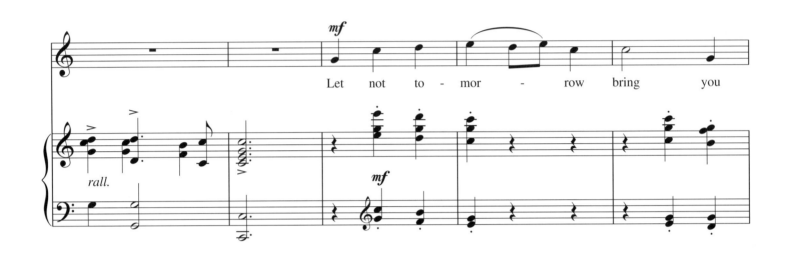

Let not to - mor - row bring you

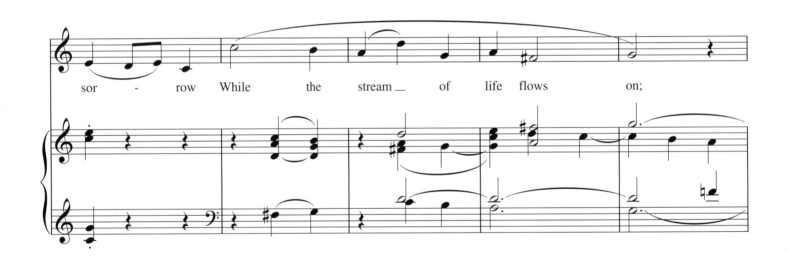

sor - row While the stream __ of life flows on;

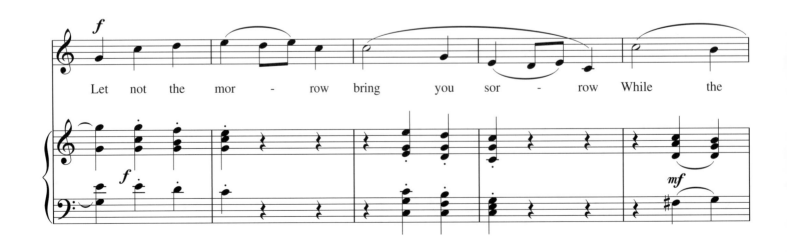

Let not the mor - row bring you sor - row While the

If you have lei - sure, fol - low pleas - ure, Let not an hour of joy pass by;

If you have lei - sure, fol - low pleas - ure, Let not an

THE DUKE OF BEDFORD

Collected and arranged by
Cecil J. Sharp

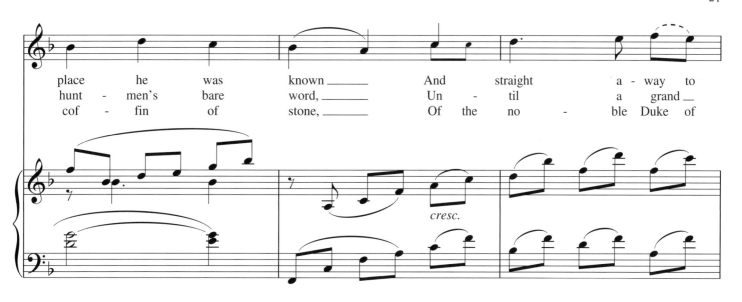

place he was known _____ And straight a - way to
hunt - men's bare word, _____ Un - til a grand __
cof - fin of stone, _____ Of the no - ble Duke of

Lon - don To the place __ he was born. 3. They o - pened his
la - dy Cried: __ 'Tis __ my dear lord. 6. She kneeled down be -
Bed - ford In his cof - fin of stone. 9. With - in Wo - burn

gar - ments And stretched out his feet, _____ And gar - nished him all
side him And kissed his cold cheek _____ And sad - ly did __
Ab - bey His bod - y was laid, _____ A - mongst _____ his __

FAREWELL, NANCY

Collected and arranged by
Cecil J. Sharp

Andante

1. Fare - well, my dear - est Nan - cy, since
3. Your pret - ty lit - tle hands can't

I must now leave you; Un - to the salt seas I am
han - dle our tack - le, And your pret - ty lit - tle feet on our

bound for to go; But let my long ab - sence be
top - mast can't go; And the cold storm - y weath - er, Love, you

no trou - ble ____ to you, For ____ I shall re -
ne'er can ____ en - dure, ____ There - fore, dear - est

turn in the spring, ___ as you ___ know.
Nan - cy, to the seas ___ do not ___ go.

2. Like some pret - ty lit - tle sea - boy, I will
4. So fare - well, my dear - est Nan - cy, since ___

dress and go ___ with you; In the deep - est of ___
I must now ___ leave you; Un - to the salt ___

f

marcato

GENTLE ANNIE

Stephen C. Foster

Moderately slow

mp *expressively*

1. Thou wilt come no more, gen - tle An - nie; like a
roamed and loved 'mid the bow - ers when thy
hours grow sad while I pon - der near the

flower, thy spir - it did de - part. Thou art gone, a - las! like the
down - y cheeks were in their bloom. Now I start a - lone 'mid the
si - lent spot where thou art laid, and my heart bows down when I

man - y that have bloomed in the sum - mer of my heart.
flow - ers while they min - gle their per - fume o'er thy tomb.
wan - der by the streams and the mead - ows where we strayed.

Shall we

never more be - hold thee nev - er hear thy win-ning voice a -

gain   when the spring - time comes, gen - tle An - nie,   when the

wild   flowers are scat - tered o'er   the plain?

1, 2

3

2. We have
3. Ah! the

rit.

I AM A PIRATE KING
from *The Pirates of Penzance*

W.S. Gilbert

Arthur Sullivan

Allegro moderato

1. Oh, bet - ter far to live __ and die
2. When I sal - ly forth to seek __ my prey, I

Un - der the brave black flag I fly, Than play a sanc - ti -
help my - self in a roy - al way. I sink a few more

I WANT WHAT I WANT WHEN I WANT IT

from *Mlle. Modiste*

Henry Blossom

Victor Herbert

cursed with a shrew of a wife._____ I drink my fill, if I
would -n't suit me, not at all._____ Of course, your life, if you

p

poco meno

have the will, with friends who are tried and old,_____ And
have no wife, is lone - some at times and slow,_____ But

marcato

poco meno

a tempo

oft, when the com - pa - ny's good, I stay; I may not come home till the
wheth - er you mar - ry or not, they say, You're bound to re - gret___ it

a tempo

accel.   *rit.*

break of day, But if din - ner is wait - ing and I am a - way, There is
ei - ther way; Let those who are sin - gle be sor - ry who may, I'd be

p accel.   *rit.*

THE LAW IS THE TRUE EMBODIMENT
from *Iolanthe*

W.S. Gilbert

Arthur Sullivan

rath-er sus-cep-ti-ble Chan - cel-lor!

ff

But though the com - pli - ment im-plied In - flates me with le -

p

git - i - mate pride, It nev - er - the-less can't be de-nied, That it has its in - con-

ven - i - ent side. For I'm not so old, and not so plain, And I'm

THE MIDSHIPMITE

Fred E. Weatherly

Stephen Adams

1. 'Twas in fif - ty - five, on a
2. We launched the cut - ter, an'
3. "I'm done for now; good -

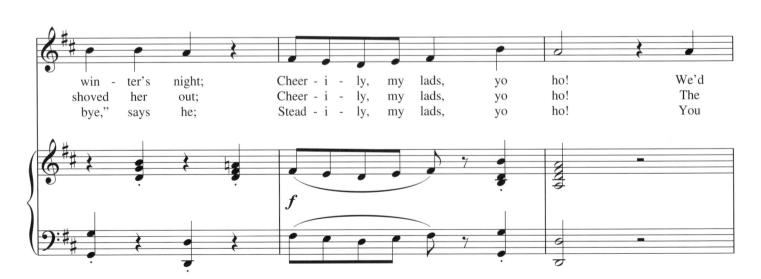

win - ter's night; Cheer - i - ly, my lads, yo ho! We'd
shoved her out; Cheer - i - ly, my lads, yo ho! The
bye," says he; Stead - i - ly, my lads, yo ho! You

got the Roosh - an lines in sight, When _ up comes a lit - tle
lub - bers might ha' heard us shout, As the Mid - dy ___ cried, "Now, my
make for the boat, nev - er mind for me!" "We'll _ take 'ee ___ back, sir, or

Mid - ship - mite; Cheer - i - ly, my lads, yo ho! — _
lads, put a -bout;" Cheer - i - ly, my lads, yo ho! We
die," says we; Cheer - i - ly, my lads, yo ho! So we

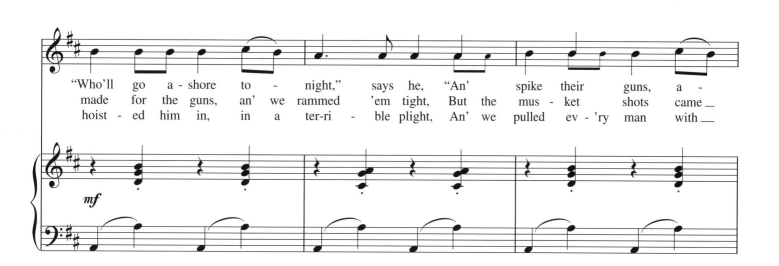

"Who'll go a -shore to - night," says he, "An' spike their guns, a -
made for the guns, an' we rammed 'em tight, But the mus - ket shots came _
hoist - ed him in, in a ter-ri - ble plight, An' we pulled ev -'ry man with _

long wi' me?" "Why, __ bless 'ee, __ sir! come a - long," says we;
left and right, An' __ down drops the poor lit - tle Mid - ship - mite;
all his might, An' __ saved the __ poor lit - tle Mid - ship - mite;

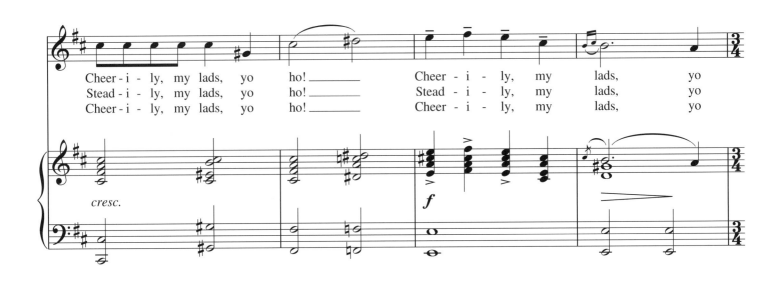

Cheer - i - ly, my lads, yo ho! _____ Cheer - i - ly, my lads, yo
Stead - i - ly, my lads, yo ho! _____ Stead - i - ly, my lads, yo
Cheer - i - ly, my lads, yo ho! _____ Cheer - i - ly, my lads, yo

cresc.

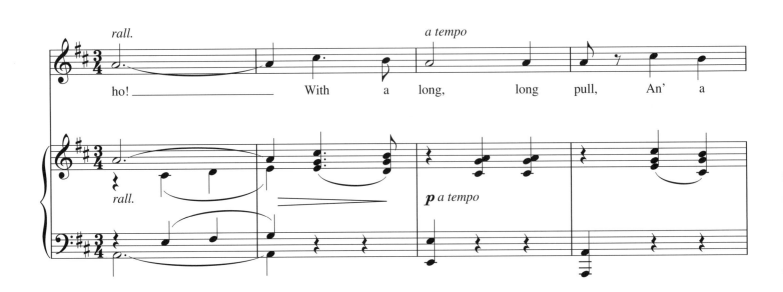

ho! _____ With a long, long pull, An' a

51

MY GENEROUS HEART DISDAINS

Francis Hopkinson

ty. I ____ scorn his ser - vile ____ chains and boast my

lib - er - ty. This whin - ing and pin - ing, And

poco rit. *a tempo*

wast - ing with care, Are ___ not ____ to my taste, Be she

ev - er so fair. This whin - ing and pin - ing, And

wast - ing with care, Are not to my taste, Be she

ev - er so fair.

55

and des - pair? Curse __ my __ for - tune __ and __ des -

pair? My __ gen' - rous heart dis - dains the __ slave of love to

be, I __ scorn his ser - vile chains, And __ boast my lib - er -

ty. I __ scorn his ser - vile __ chains, And boast my

lib - er - ty. This whin-ing and pin-ing, And wast - ing with

care, Are — not — to my taste, Be she ev - er so fair. This

whin-ing and pin - ing, And wast - ing with care, Are —

not — to my taste, Be she ev - er so fair!

NOTHING BUT A PLAIN OLD SOLDIER

Stephen C. Foster

60

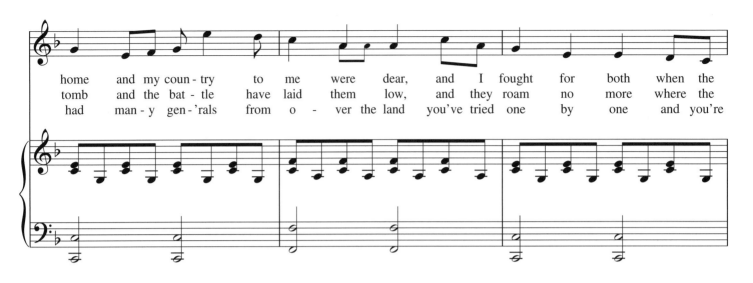

home and my coun-try to me were dear, and I fought for both when the
tomb and the bat - tle have laid them low, and they roam no more where the
had man - y gen-'rals from o - ver the land you've tried one by one and you're

ad lib.

foe came near, but now I will meet with a slight or sneer, for I'm
bright streams flow. I'm long - ing to join them and soon must go, for I'm
still at a stand, but when I took the field we had one in com- mand, yet I'm

colla voce

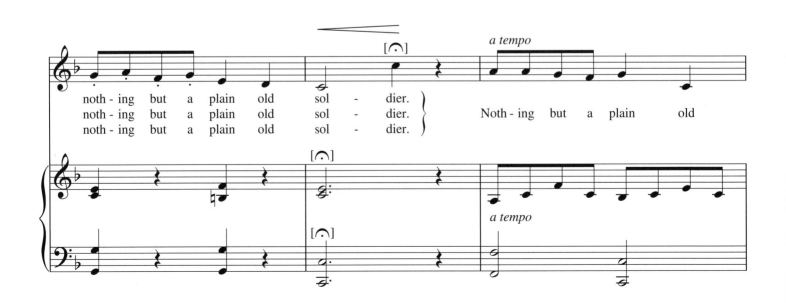

[𝄐]   *a tempo*

noth - ing but a plain old sol - dier.
noth - ing but a plain old sol - dier. Noth - ing but a plain old
noth - ing but a plain old sol - dier.

[𝄐]

a tempo

soldier, an old revolutionary soldier, but I've

handled a gun where noble deeds were done, for the name of my commander was

George Washington.

1, 2

3

2. The
3. A -

THE OLD ROAD

Reginald V. Darow

John Prindle Scott

Straight and white, in the hot sun light, The __ high road stretch - es far; I hear the beat of the tramp - ing feet, Where the man - y trav - el - ers are; But my thoughts to - day fly

far, far a-way To a lit-tle wind-ing road, I knew, For my road is the old road, Where the sun lies warm and still, And my road is a by-road That winds up o-ver a hill; O, the high road is a long road, Where the

wear - y way - far - ers roam; But I will take that lit - tle

wind - ing road That leads the wan - der - er home!

Man - y a mile I have trav - eled the while, Through man - y a vale and

town; But wear - y am I, with the night draw - ing nigh, When the

sun is go - ing down! But on I'll go through the af - ter glow, Till the

old cross - roads I see. For my road is the

old road, That my fa - thers used to climb, And

my road is a by - road That I took in the old - en

time! O, the high road is a long road, Where the

cresc. wear - y way - far - ers roam; *f* But I will take that lit - tle

rit. *allarg.* wind - ing road That leads the wan - der - er home!

PUNCHINELLO

Fred E. Weatherly

James L. Molloy

He was a Pun - chi - nel - lo, Sweet Col - um - bine was she,
Bright was the day she mar - ried, And there a - mong the rest,

He loved the ground she danced on. She laughed his love to see;
Came poor old Pun - chi - nel - lo He was the blith - est guest.

68

THE RAMBLING SAILOR

Collected and arranged by
Cecil J. Sharp

Moderato

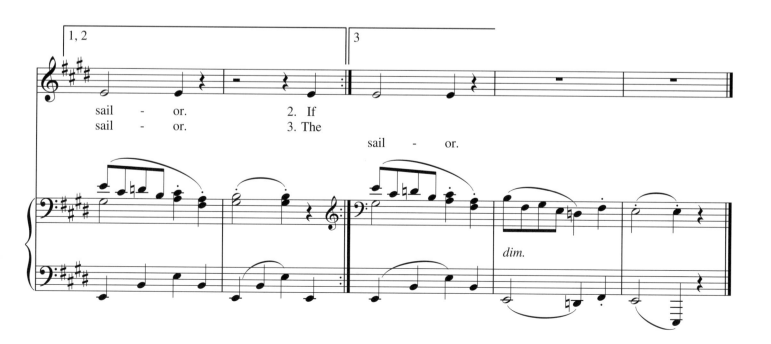

SHIPMATES O' MINE

Edward Teschemacher

Wilfred Sanderson

Maestoso

"Forth to the new land that ev - er is call - ing!" For - tune at - tend you there!

Good luck go with you! Ship - mates _____ o' mine!

Tell me, tell me, where are you roam - ing, Ship - mates o'

mine? O'er blue seas or where the grey waves are foam - ing,

Ship - mates __ o' mine? Nev - er a mes - sage, oh!

dim. *p*

tell us your sto - ry, All Fate has giv'n you, sor - row or glo - ry;

marcato *rit.* *f*

Send us one word, for our lone hearts are wait - ing, Ship - mates _____ o'

pesante *rit.* *sf sf sf sf*

THE SONG OF BROTHER HILARIO

Stephen Chalmers

Ralph Cox

mp *più lento e sostenuto*

I like to dream by the qui - et __ stream, Where the

mp
più lento e sostenuto

sim - ple wa - ters flow. I love the knell of the ves - per __ bell, When the

sink - ing sun __ lies low. I like to think, when my day is dead, And the

night falls __ dark and deep, That this sweet earth shall be __ my __ bed, When I

rit.

rit.

THREE POOR MARINERS

Words Anonymous

Old English Melody
arranged by
Roger Quilter

Maestoso e poco più moderato

We care not for those mar - tial men That

do ___ our states dis - dain, But we care for those

mar - chant men ___ Who do our states main - tain. So

WHILE THE FOAMING BILLOWS ROLL

Thomas Linley

H. Lane Wilson

"Come, come, my jol - ly lads, the wind's a - baft, Brisk gales our sails shall crowd; Come come, my jol - ly lads, now haul the boat," The bo' - s'un _ pipes a - loud. The _ ship's un - moored, all

rall.　　　*a tempo*

Though to the Span-ish coast we're bound to steer, We'll still our rights main -

mf

tain, Then bear a hand, be stead-y, boys, Soon we'll see Old Eng - land _ once a -

cresc.　　　　　　　　　　　　　　　*f*

gain. From _ shore to shore, while can - nons

cresc.　　　　　　　　　*f*　　*ff*